The
Science of a
Light Bulb

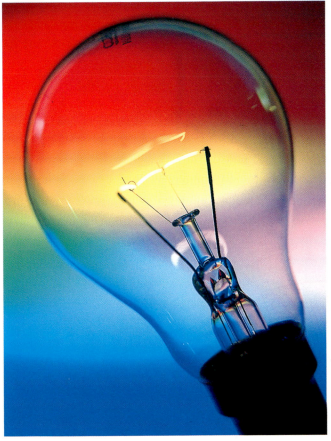

Neville Evans

RSVP
RAINTREE
STECK-VAUGHN
PUBLISHERS
A Steck-Vaughn Company

Austin, Texas
www.steck-vaughn.com

Science World

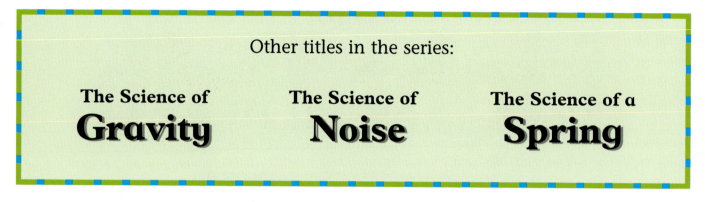

Other titles in the series:

The Science of
Gravity

The Science of
Noise

The Science of a
Spring

Picture acknowledgments
The publishers would like to thank the following for allowing their pictures to be reproduced in this book: Martyn F. Chillmaid 8 [top], 13 [bottom]; Eye Ubiquitous/N. Holden 7 [bottom]; Getty Images/Warren Bolster 4, /Ken Briggs 5, /Chad Ehlers 22, /Steven Johnson 16, /H. Richard Johnston 10, /Lenny Kalfus 17 [bottom], /Dennis O'Clair 17 [bottom middle], /Steve Taylor 17 [top middle], 21, 29 [top], /Tek Image *title page*, /Mike Timo 6; Robert Harding *cover* [main], 9 [top], 24, /Louise Murray 26 [top], /Trevor Wood 14; National Portrait Gallery 11; Popperfoto 12, 27 [bottom]; Science Photo Library 13 [top], 15 [both], 23 [top], /Martin Bond 24 [top], 26 [bottom], /Linda Phillips 17 [top], /Charles D. Winters 25; The Stock Market 7 [top], /Roger Ball 23 [bottom]; Trip/A. Lambert 8 [bottom], /Y. Philimoner 11, /H. Rogers 28 [top], /Streano/Havens 27 [top]; Wayland Picture Library *contents page*, *cover* [top and middle], 9 [bottom], 19 [top], 28 [bottom], 29 [bottom].
The chapter logo illustration is by Peter Bull.

Published by Raintree Steck-Vaughn Publishers, an imprint of Steck-Vaughn Company

Printed in Italy. Bound in the United States.
1 2 3 4 5 6 7 8 9 0 04 03 02 01 00

Library of Congress Cataloging-in-Publication Data
Evans, Neville.
The science of a light bulb / Neville Evans
    p.   cm.—(Science world)
Includes bibliographical references and index.
Summary: Traces the development of different forms of artificial lighting as well as basic information about electricity.
ISBN 0-7398-1325-0
1. Light—Juvenile literature.
2. Electricity—Juvenile literature.
3. Light bulbs—Juvenile literature.
[1. Lighting. 2. Electricity. 3. Light bulbs.]
I. Title. II. Series.
QC360.E8   2000
621.32'6—dc21   99-37299

Contents

Light Before Light Bulbs

When you go into a dark place, what do you look for first? You look for a light switch to turn on a light. Every day you use light bulbs to give instant light at the touch of a switch. At night you are surrounded by the glow of light bulbs in every building and street. Yet, just over a hundred years ago, light bulbs had not been invented. People had to make light in different ways.

▼ The sun provides us with light and warmth. The sun is a star. Stars make their own heat and light that can travel long distances through space.

Every day has two parts: light and dark, or day and night. At night we can see many different kinds of electric lights.

Long ago, when the sun went down, there was hardly any light to be seen. Sometimes there was light from the moon. Night was dark, and nobody could see. In many places of the world, it was very, very cold. Heat and light would only come the next day with the rising sun.

▲ The moon does not make its own light, like a star. The light on the moon's surface is really reflected sunlight. The light from the sun shines on the moon's surface. Then it bounces down to the earth.

Burning light

For a long time, people lived using only the sun and moon for light. Then someone, somewhere, at some time, discovered how to make fire. Fire kept people warm, even when it was dark. People found that fire gave them some light to see during the night. Light from a fire is not as good as sunlight. But it is a lot better than sitting in the dark.

▼ At night controlled fires are still used on camp sites to give people heat and light.

For many centuries people made light by burning materials. The most available thing to burn was wood cut from the surrounding trees.

However, people wanted to move around safely in the dark. But wood fires had to stay in one place. No one knew how to carry fire. People soon solved this problem. They tied wood or other materials, such as cloth or fat, onto sticks. They held them above their heads as they walked. These were called torches.

At the start of the Olympic ▶ Games, an athlete lights a torch. It burns day and night until the games finish.

What happens to different materials when a fire gets very hot?

Blacksmiths make horseshoes and gates out of iron. Iron can be bent into shape when it softens and glows red hot in a fire. When the iron cools, the metal becomes hard again. The color of burning wood becomes bright red, too. Finally, it breaks down and becomes ash. Materials such as paper and cloth break up into fine ash. But metals stay solid (but soften) and change color.

Lamps

Slowly people began to learn about other materials. They learned to burn oil and wax from plants and animals to give light. They learned to control how these materials burned and to keep them in containers, called lamps. The burning material could be carried safely in a lamp.

Later, people also learned how gases burn to provide heat and light. Gas lamps, gas cooking stoves, and gas fires began to be used in buildings. They gave heat and light. Today we have gas lamps and stoves to carry around for parties outside. The gas is stored and carried in very strong metal containers (sometimes called "bottles").

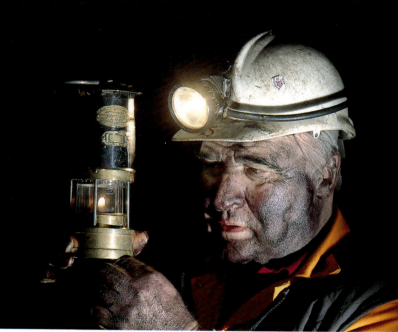

▼ Miners in the 19th century used oil lamps such as this one. They lit the dark tunnels where the miners worked. Miners now use electric lights.

Which gases are used in gas lamps and stoves?

Butane and propane are the gases used for camping stoves (right) and lights. These gases come from oil in the earth. We get many other useful materials, such as gasoline and diesel fuel, from oil. All these useful materials are taken out of oil in a place called an oil refinery.

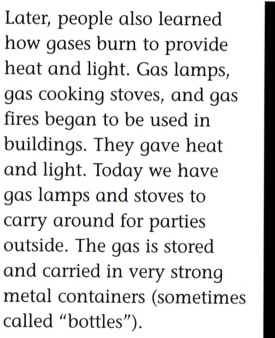

Electricity and Light

The electric lamp was invented in 1879. Several people tried to make light using electricity. They knew how lightning during thunderstorms lit up the sky with brilliant flashes of electric light. Some people tried to make the same effect in laboratories.

In the United States, Benjamin Franklin studied lightning. To lead, or conduct, electricity to the ground, he flew a kite into a thundercloud. Large, dangerous voltages of electricity traveled down the kite string to the ground. Once the electricity hit the ground, it was no longer dangerous. From this experiment Franklin invented lightning rods to protect buildings from the effects of lightning.

▲ Lightning is an electric flash of light made during a thunderstorm.

Benjamin Franklin

Benjamin Franklin (1706–1790) was an American scientist, statesman, and inventor. Today he is best remembered for his invention of lightning rods. These are rods of metal fixed to buildings and to the ground with cables. They protect the buildings by "attracting" and conducting the electricity from lightning safely down to the ground.

The arc lamp

In 1807 a young scientist named Humphry Davy invented the arc lamp. This was one successful try at making lightning. People called it "lightning on earth." The arc lamp worked by passing an electric current through two pieces of carbon, a woodlike material. When the pieces of carbon came close together, they made a bright light.

The arc lamp was very dirty. It gave off a lot of smoke and gases. Sometimes it would suddenly stop, plunging everyone into darkness. Yet arc lamps did give out very bright light.

The basic idea of an arc lamp

arc of electricity fills the gap

carbon (charcoal)

carbon (charcoal)

+

—

Battery

The electric current from a battery must be powerful enough. And the space between the carbon pieces must be small enough. Then an arc of electricity will jump across the space making a bridge of bright light.

◀ Lighthouses used arc lamps until the 1920s. Some had arc lamps and mirrors to reflect more light out into the sea. Today lighthouses use powerful electric-filament bulbs, which last longer and work better.

Arc lamps provided ▶ street lighting in many European and American cities in the late 19th century. They were then replaced by electric-filament bulbs.

Sir Humphry Davy

Humphry Davy (1778–1829) was a brilliant chemist who lived in London. He loved experimenting with metals and gases. As well as the electric arc lamp, he also invented the Davy safety lamp. It was for use by miners underground. Miners were afraid of lighting dangerous gases with flames and causing them to blow up. The safety lamp covered the flame with a wire mesh to keep the gases from being lit. Humphry Davy was also a poet and a popular public speaker.

Problems to be solved

No one could depend on an arc lamp to produce bright light for long. Many scientists around the world tried to find other ways of making bright light using electricity.

Thomas Alva Edison

Thomas Alva Edison (1847–1931) was the most famous American inventor to experiment with electric light. He discovered that when he joined materials to a battery, they usually heated up. If he used more batteries, and more power, the materials would become red. Sometimes they even became white with heat. But the materials lasted only a short time before they broke up. Edison tried using different materials, such as paper, wood, and even corn! He found that metals lasted longer than other materials.

Sir Joseph Wilson Swan

Sir Joseph Wilson Swan (1828–1914), was an English chemist who experimented with electric light. His designs influenced Edison's final bulbs. Both Edison and Swan set up companies to provide electric lighting throughout their countries. Swan also made important inventions in photography.

The first problem for the scientists was that their electric lamps worked just sometimes. At one moment there would be bright light, the next moment darkness. These lamps would be of no use for houses and streets. They would need to be checked all the time.

The main part of the lamp was the metal carrying the electric current. It was exposed to the open air, which made it burn faster. So the light didn't last long. How could this problem be solved? Simple, cover the metal up! But surely if it was covered up, the light wouldn't be seen though. But the cover could be made of something like glass that the light could go through. Then the light would be seen.

Materials that let light ▶ through, such as glass and some plastics, are called transparent. Can you think of any glass objects that you look through? For example, you can look through windows and glass over pictures.

Edison's glass bulb

Edison decided to experiment with lighting metal materials inside a glass bulb. He hoped that the bulb would make the hot metal give light longer.

Edison was right. It did work much better, but the design still needed a lot of work. The inside of the bulb became very black—not much use for letting light through. He worked more on the problem.

Edison tried many times but failed. He then wondered whether the air inside the bulb was part of the problem. When the metal in the bulb got hot, the air helped it to burn. So Edison pumped most of the air from inside the bulb. And the metal burned more slowly. The light lasted for a longer time. This was the first step to an electric light bulb that worked.

▼ People have made objects by heating and softening glass for many years.

Success!

Finally, in 1879, Edison made an electric lamp
that stayed on for several minutes. He was
highly delighted. Can you imagine anyone
being happy about a light that stayed on for
only a few minutes? Today we have lights that
stay on for days.

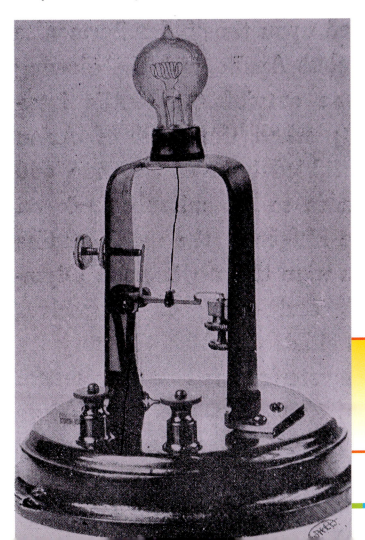

No one before Edison had ever got a
lamp to stay lighted for more than a
few minutes. Without Edison's and
Swan's work, we might not have
light bulbs that really work well.

Filaments

Edison found that thick pieces of metal did not work for his bulbs. Instead, he made the metal very thin, as thin as a piece of thread. These pieces of metal are called filaments, from the Latin word for *thread*. Edison's electric-filament bulbs are still in use today, all over the world.

Electric-filament bulbs ▶ are often called incandescent from the Latin word for "being white." The light from the filament glows white when hot.

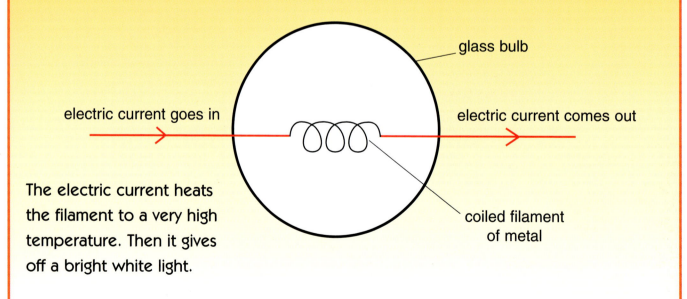

A simple plan of how an electric-filament bulb lights

glass bulb

electric current goes in

electric current comes out

The electric current heats the filament to a very high temperature. Then it gives off a bright white light.

coiled filament of metal

Before scientists found the perfect filament for Edison's bulb, they had many questions to answer. Today we know the answers to the questions:

Q. Which metal should a filament be made from?
A. The best metal to use is called tungsten. It makes a very bright white light and doesn't melt as soon as other metals.

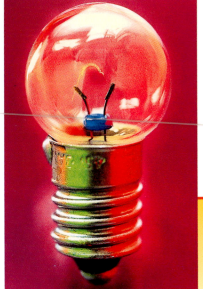

Q. Is a straight filament better or worse than a coiled filament?
A. A coiled filament is better than a straight one because it lasts longer.

Q. How hot should a filament be?
A. The filament needs to be at a temperature of more than 2,000° C.

Q. Would it be better to have a small amount of gas inside a bulb or no gas at all?
A. It is better to have a small amount of the gases argon and nitrogen inside a bulb. These gases prevent the filament from burning up too fast.

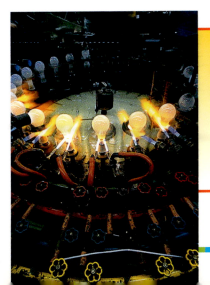

Electric circuits

All electrical articles in your house can be plugged into outlets in the walls. Behind the walls are wires joined to each other. They are also joined to the electricity supply, which makes the electric switches work. This system of wires with the electricity supply is called an electric circuit.

Light bulbs, switches, and electricity are all linked together. To understand how, look at simple electric circuits.

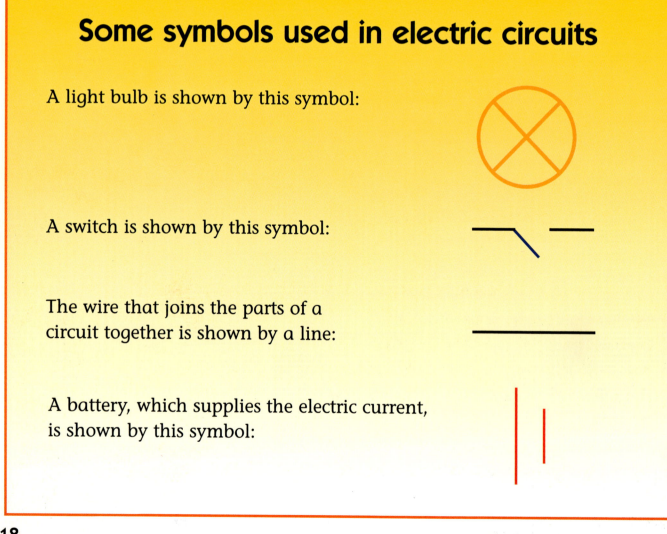

Some symbols used in electric circuits

A light bulb is shown by this symbol:

A switch is shown by this symbol:

The wire that joins the parts of a circuit together is shown by a line:

A battery, which supplies the electric current, is shown by this symbol:

The simplest circuit is this one:

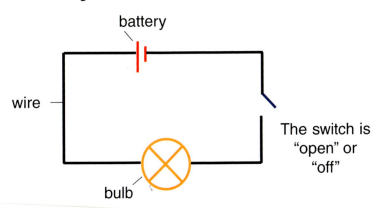

battery

wire

bulb

The switch is "open" or "off"

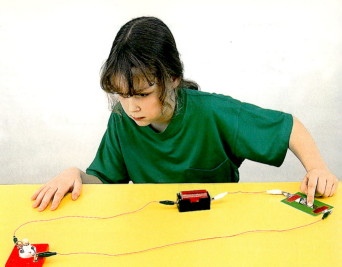

The switch is open (off), so there is a gap, or break, in the circuit. The gap is too large for the electric current to jump across. So there is no flow of electricity through the bulb and therefore no light.

▲ If you make a simple circuit and press the switch on, the bulb will light.

What are voltage numbers?

Voltage numbers indicate the electric "strength," e.g. 2 volt, or 2V, of an object. Each battery and bulb has a voltage number. The voltage numbers on the bulb and battery must be the same. If not, the bulb will not light. The battery voltage may be much lower than the bulb needs. Then the filament of the bulb will only glow a dull red. The battery voltage may be higher. Then the filament will glow a bright white for a short time. Then it will break and be of no further use.

Modern Lighting

Today we have many different kinds of lights. These lights are not natural, like sunlight. They are made by people or machines in factories. These lights are not as good as sunlight. But their use over the past century has changed everyday life for the better. We use lights for many reasons. They help us to drive and walk safely at night, read, shop, and light buildings. They even help us to see in refrigerators.

Think about all the hundreds or even thousands of lights you see at night in a city. For these lights to work at the same time, a special system is used. It makes the needed electricity. No battery is big enough. The electricity comes from an electric generator in a power plant.

▼ The glow of thousands of lights all over this city is made by electricity from a power plant.

Michael Faraday

Michael Faraday (1791–1867) worked on electromagnetism and other sciences at The Royal Institution, London. He was a very intelligent scientist but a little shy. However, he loved speaking to groups of young people. Without his discoveries of electromagnetism, none of the lighting systems we depend on today would be possible.

The generator works because there is a close link between electricity and magnetism, called electromagnetism. Most of the early research on this topic was done by Michael Faraday. He later became known as "the father of electricity." Faraday discovered what happens when a coil of wire spins fast between the poles of a magnet. Big voltages and large electric currents are made. This is electromagnetism.

These men are inspecting the blades ▶ of a generator. Generators are large machines in a power plant. They are forced by the motion of steam or water to spin around very fast. This makes the large voltages of electricity that power our homes.

How does electricity get from the power plant to my house?

The voltages generated in power plants are so high and dangerous that they have to be carried to the surrounding towns by thick cables. You have probably seen large metal towers, called pylons (right), which carry electric cables. In cities, electric cables are also covered by insulating material (to keep the electricity from passing through the cable into anything or anyone touching it) and buried underground.

Most lights in houses still use Edison's kind of electric light. That light is a very hot filament inside a glass bulb. However, they have one problem. They make a lot of heat as well as light. In nature, when you get light, you get heat. Think about fires, or the sun. The heat given off by a light bulb is wasted. It doesn't help you see any better.

Fluorescent lighting

In the 1950s, after a lot of experimenting, scientists developed a new kind of electric light. It was called a fluorescent tube. This new long and thin light didn't look at all like the first light bulbs. The glass tube was filled with gases and didn't need a metal filament. There are usually two gases inside the tube—argon and mercury vapor.

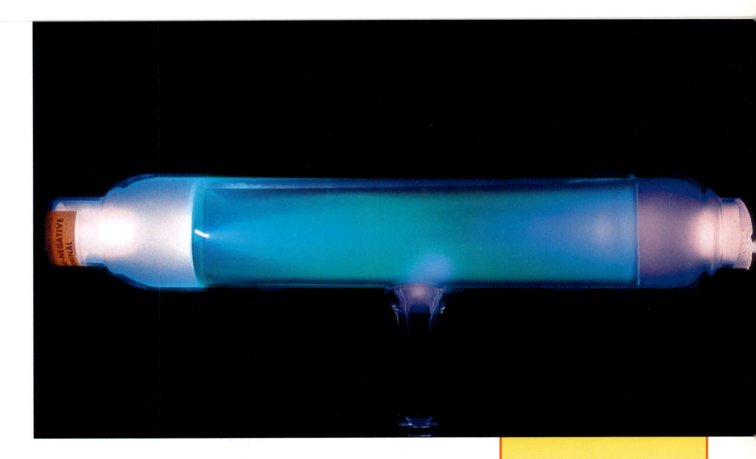

In order to make the light even brighter, the inside surface of the tube is painted. It is coated with a material called phosphor. Some people have described fluorescent lighting as "lightning in a bottle." Look for fluorescent tube lighting around you today. You will see it in many places.

▲ Fluorescent lights can be different colors. It depends on what type of gas is used in each tube.

Fluorescent tube lights are very useful. They don't get as hot as filament lights using the same power. This means they do not drain as much energy from a power plant. They are also much cheaper to use than filament bulbs. Modern fluorescent lights are all designed to save energy in homes and in workplaces. They last eight times longer than filament bulbs but make the same amount of light.

These modern fluorescent lights ▶ show how the design of the long, thin tubes 50 years ago has changed. The tubes have become smaller and can be used in the same fittings as filament bulbs.

One filament or fluorescent light gives a lot of light. It is useful in small spaces, such as rooms in a house or beside your bed. But one light does not give enough light to cover longer distances. So several lights are needed on streets or along halls. For greater brightness, other kinds of lights are needed. These lights are used in stadiums, large parking lots, hospital operating rooms, television studios, and in lighthouses. Their brightness is needed to make places safe or to give a clear picture of small things. Some lights need to be seen from a long way away.

All electric lamps were developed from the filament or arc lamp. So we owe thanks to all the scientists who helped invent our modern lighting.

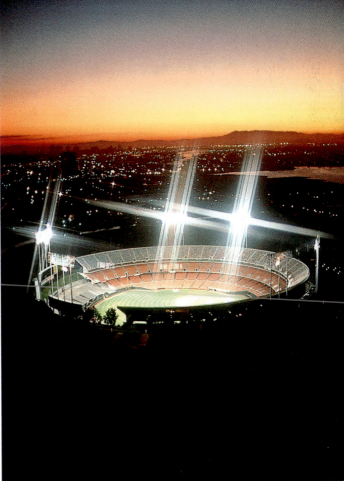

▲ Very powerful lights are needed to light stadiums. Though they light just the inside of the stadium, people can see the lights from far away.

◀ Many lights are needed to light up long halls. This exhibition center is using many different lights to decorate the hallway.

More Points About Light

1. Light starts out from something. We call this a source. The biggest source that we are familiar with is our sun.

Warning!

Never look directly at the sun, especially with binoculars or a telescope. The sun's light is so strong that it could hurt your eyes very badly.

2. Light from a source travels in all directions. If we are to see, the light must travel into our eyes.

3. Our eyes are not sources of light. Light goes into our eyes. There has to be light so that they can see anything. Our eyes cannot see in total darkness.

4. Other sources of light are electric lights, candles, and fires. Some living creatures, such as fireflies, make their own light.

5. Light from sources travels around and hits objects in the way. Sometimes it goes through the object, if the object is transparent. All these objects are transparent.

6. If an object is not transparent, it is called opaque. Light "bounces off" opaque objects. (This is sometimes called reflection and sometimes scattering.)

7. "Bouncing off" allows us to see things. This is how you are able to read this sentence. The light from some sources (the sun in daytime, a lamp at night) hits this page. It then "bounces off" into your eye.

8. Reflections—in very special cases, the effect of "bouncing off" is shocking. You can see yourself in a surface if it is shiny, like a mirror. You can have a lot of fun using mirrors of different kinds. Silvery or shiny surfaces are best for making reflections. Any shiny surface will do. Look around for some and then look at your reflection in them.

Glossary

Battery An object that can store electricity and can be used to power things that run on electricity.

Circuits The paths of electric currents.

Conduct To lead or guide.

Electric currents The flow of electricity through, for example, a wire.

Electricity An invisible form of energy that is used to make light and heat, and to power machines.

Electromagnetism Energy that is made of electricity and magnetic energies.

Energy The power to make things work.

Filament A thread-like piece of metal used in a light bulb. It gives light when an electric current passes through it.

Gases Materials that are neither solid nor liquid, like oxygen in air. Some gases burn to make heat and light.

Generator A machine that makes electric power.

Insulating Covering bare electrical wire with a material, e.g., plastic or rubber, that electricity will not pass through and will not harm anyone touching it.

Laboratories Places where scientists carry out experiments.

Lightning A large electric flash of light made during a thunderstorm.

Miners People who work underground to dig out materials such as coal.

Natural Having something to do with nature; not made by humans.

Oil refinery A place where oil is separated into several pure forms, such as gasoline and diesel fuel.

Opaque Not letting light pass through. The opposite of transparent.

Reflected Thrown back, as when light has bounced off an opaque object.

Socket A hole or hollow place that something is fitted into, e.g., an electric light socket.

Stoves Metal objects that can give heat for cooking or for warming a room.

Switch A small lever or handle that turns an electric current on or off.

Vapor The gas form of a material that is usually solid or liquid, e.g., mercury.

Volt The unit used for measuring the force of electricity.

Voltage The strength of electrical power, measured in volts.

Further Information

Books to read

Berger, Samantha. *Electricity* (Science Emergent Readers). New York: Scholastic, 1999.

Flaherty, Michael. *Electricity and Batteries* (Science Factory). Providence, RI: Copper Beech, 1999.

Linder, Greg. *Thomas Edison: A Photo-Illustrated Biography* (Photo-Illustrated Biographies). Mankato, MN: Bridgestone Books, 1999.

Middleton, Haydn. *Thomas Edison: The Wizard Inventor* (What's Their Story?) New York: Oxford University Press, 1997.

Oxlade, Chris. *Electricty and Magnetism* (Science Topics). Portsmouth, NH: Heinemann, 1999.

Websites to visit

ericir.syr.edu/Projects/Newton/newtonalpha
This site contains many interesting science lessons.

www.lsc.org
This is the home page of the Liberty Science Center.

www.discoveryplace.org
This is the home page of Discovery Place.

www-hpcc.asto.washington.edu/ scied/museum.html
This site has links to many science museums.

Places to visit

Liberty Science Center, Liberty State Park, Phillip Street, Jersey City, NJ (Tel: 201-200-1000). This outstanding science museum has hands-on activities guided by the museum staff.

Discovery Place, 301 North Tryon Street, Charlotte, NC (Tel: 1-800-935-0553). This is an award-winning science and technology museum, featuring hands-on experiments. See "websites to visit" (above) for information on where to find your nearest hands-on science center.

Index

Numbers in **bold** refer to pictures as well as text.